TOOLBOX

TOOLBOX TRAINING *presents*

100 NATURE ACTIVITIES FOR KIDS

assembled and edited by David L. Whitaker

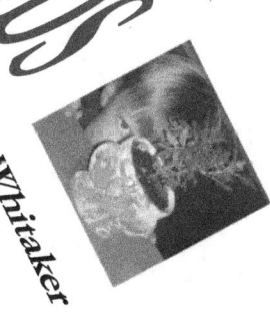

100 Nature Activities for Kids

These activities focus on rocks, leaves, plants, animals, and other aspects of the outdoors. On many of the projects, kids can observe and experiment. Some activities bring in an art element while others, such as the camping activities, lend themselves to dramatic play. These 100 activities have been compiled and edited with school-agers (5-12 years old) in mind, but can be adapted to other ages. They are divided into the following categories:

These activities have been compiled over many years time from many formal and informal sources. Every attempt has been made to credit original sources, but if you find an activity that needs a resource cited, let Toolbox Training know!

For more about additional books, or other **TOOLBOX TRAINING** products and services, check out the information below.

TOOLBOX TRAINING
www.toolboxtrainingonline.com
Phone: 913.789.9733 **E-mail:** toolboxtraining@yahoo.com
Facebook: www.facebook.com/toolboxtraining

WEATHER

WEATHER:
Cloud Watching (A1)

Materials:

☐ Paper

☐ Small notebooks (optional)

☐ Writing utensils

☐ Binoculars

Directions:

1. Keep sky journals of observations of the clouds.

2. Children can study the different types of clouds and see how they are different.

3. Kids can also try to predict the weather based on the different clouds.

4. They may wish to get some books from your local library about clouds to help them.

5. Kids can also sketch clouds or write poetry about them.

6. Of course, they can also just lay on their backs and look for different shapes within the clouds.

Source: Adapted from Kathleen Carroll's *A Guide to Great Field Trips* (2007 Zephyr Press)

WEATHER:
Clouds in a Bottle (A2)

Materials:

- Large glass jar with a wide mouth (such as an industrial size pickle jar)
- Sheet of rubber (such as a balloon that is slit open)
- Cold water
- Book to cover mouth of jar
- Chalk dust or talcum powder
- Spoon
- Rubber band

Directions:

1. Wash the jar and put about an inch of water in the bottom.

2. Cover the mouth of the jar with the rubber. Cover with a book to hold it in place.

3. After 10-15 minutes, remove the book and rubber from the jar.

4. Drop in a spoonful of chalk dust or talcum powder and quickly replace the rubber over the mouth.

5. Wrap the rubber band tightly around the rim of the jar to keep the rubber in place.

6. Push down on the rubber with fist until it is depressed a little way into the jar.

7. After 15 seconds or so, remove fist and a cloud will form inside the jar.

Source: http://bizarrelabs.com/cloudb.htm

WEATHER:
Weather Calendar (A3)

Materials:

- ❏ 2 large calendars or poster board to make calendars
- ❏ construction paper
- ❏ ruler
- ❏ pencil
- ❏ glue
- ❏ scissors
- ❏ markers

Directions:

1. Discuss weather conditions with the children. What's the weather going to be like today? How can we find out?

2. The children will cut out symbols from construction paper that describe the weather (such as an umbrella for a rainy day, sun for a sunny day, or cloud for a cloudy day).

3. The children can also write the days of the week and the dates on the calendar.

4. The children may want to call the weather line to get a prediction for the day.

5. The children can attach the symbol for the day and write in the temperature.

WEATHER:
Cricket Thermometer (A4)

Materials:

- [ ] live cricket
- [ ] a watch with a secondhand
- [ ] jar
- [ ] nylon stocking
- [ ] rubber band

Directions:

1. This works best outside in warm weather.

2. Catch a cricket and place it in a jar.

3. Stretch the stocking over the top of the jar and secure with a rubber band.

4. Count the cricket chirps in 15 seconds.

5. Add 40 to the number of chirps counted.

6. The total sum equals the air temperature in degrees Fahrenheit around the cricket.

7. Check the temperature with the weather report.

8. Repeat several times before releasing cricket.

WEATHER:
Straw Weather Vane (A5)

Materials:

- pencil
- clay
- straw
- scissors
- glue

- straight pin
- ruler
- construction paper
- square piece of cardboard
- bead

Directions:

1. Use construction paper and cut two end pieces for the arrow.

2. Cut slits into each end of the straw and insert the two pieces and glue.

3. Stick the straight pin through the straw, the bead, and into the pencil eraser.

4. Rotate around until the straw turns freely.

5. A small piece of clay may need to be put on the straw to balance it.

6. Draw two cross lines on the cardboard piece and label them N, S, E, W.

7. Put a lump of clay in the middle of the cardboard piece and push pencil into clay.

8. Go outside and point the N on the cardboard to the North. Which direction is the wind blowing?

WEATHER:
Wire Hanger Weather Vane (A6)

Materials:

- wire coat hanger
- aluminum foil
- tape
- pint-sized plastic tub and lid
- sand
- scissors
- markers

Directions:

1. Bend the loop of a coat hanger so that it is as straight as possible.

2. Cover half of the coat hanger with foil and use tape to secure edges around the hanger.

3. Fill the plastic tube completely with sand, packing it tightly. Put on the lid.

4. Poke a hole in the center of the lid and push straight part of coat hanger into lid.

5. The vane should turn freely. If not, check size of hole in lid to assure it is big enough.

6. Using markers or crayons, mark N, S, E, and W on sides of container.

7. Place outside with N pointing north. Which way is the wind coming from?

WEATHER:
Rain Gauge (A7)

Materials:

❑ clear jar with straight sides   ❑ ruler

Directions:

1. Use a ruler to measure several inches on the side of a clear jar.

2. Mark measurements with fingernail polish.

3. The scale may be marked in inches with quarter-inches visible.

4. Place the rain gauge in an open area and check daily for any amount of precipitation.

WEATHER:
Barometer (A8)

Materials:

- coffee can
- large balloon
- rubber band
- 9" x 6" poster board

- small drinking straw
- tape
- markers
- resource books

Directions:

1. Cut the balloon to fit over the top of the coffee can. Secure the balloon tightly with a rubber band.

2. Cut one end of a straw to form a point.

3. Tape the other end to the balloon with the pointed end hanging off the can's edge.

4. Use the poster board to make a sign. Print "barometer" at the top.

5. Tape the sign to the back of the can.

6. Above the straw pointer print "high" and below it print "low."

7. Observe any movement in the straw from day to day.

8. Have resource materials for children to find out what it means when the straw moves. Also, a commercial barometer is handy to have to compare results.

WEATHER:
Human Hair Hygrometer (A9)

Materials:

- ❑ strand of human hair
- ❑ toothpick
- ❑ glue

- ❑ pipe cleaner
- ❑ clear, wide-mouth glass of jar
- ❑ markers

Directions:

1. Pluck a single strand of hair a few inches longer than the glass is tall. Try different colors of hair to see which will work best.

2. Wrap one end of the hair around the center of a toothpick a few times. Add a drop of glue to secure it in place.

3. Color one end of the toothpick with a marker.

4. Bend the pipe cleaner at both ends to form a yoke and place it across the top of the glass.

5. Hold the toothpick by the hair and hang it inside the jar. Make sure toothpick hangs just above the bottom of the jar and does not touch the sides.

6. Wrap the free end of hair around the pipe cleaner yoke. Secure with a drop of glue.

7. Notice the change in direction of the toothpick over fair and rainy weather. Using a colored marker, indicate the "rain" and "clear" positions on outside of the jar. Once set with correct markings, do not move it.

WEATHER:
Weather Station (A10)

Materials:

- ❏ thermometer
- ❏ barometer
- ❏ hygrometer
- ❏ wind vane

Directions:

1. Collect several maps from newspapers to compare daily conditions.

2. Notice the various symbols and their meanings.

3. Record daily conditions on charts and graphs.

4. Make signs to label all homemade instruments. Include explanations of what the instrument does and how it works.

5. You can put these instruments and charts on display after you have completed the charts and graphs for whatever time period you wish. (week, month, etc.)

ENVIRONMENT

ENVIRONMENT:
Is It Or Is It Not Biodegradable?
(B1)

Materials:

- apple core
- leaf of lettuce
- plastic packaging
- piece of Styrofoam
- shovel

Directions:

1. Check first to make sure there is a place that will be okay to dig holes.

2. Dig four holes. They should be just deep enough for the objects listed in the material list.

3. Put the apple core, leaf of lettuce, plastic packaging, and Styrofoam in four separate holes.

4. Fill the holes back up with dirt.

5. Mark the spots where the holes are so you will be able to find them again.

6. Wait a month and then go back and dig up all four holes.

7. What happened to the four objects?

8. Explanation: because the apple and lettuce are biodegradable, they will have partially or completely turned into soil. However, the plastic and Styrofoam should still be completely in tact - as they will be for years to come.

ENVIRONMENT:
Smog Patrol (B2)

Materials:

- eight natural rubber bands
- two coat hangers
- plastic bag
- magnifying glass

Directions:

1. Bend the coat hangers into rectangles.

2. Slide two rubber bands on to each side of each coat hanger. Each coat hanger will have four rubber bands on it, two on each side of the hook part of the hanger.

3. Hang one hanger outside. It is important that it is in a shady place out of the sun.

4. Put the other coat hanger in a plastic bag and seal it tightly. Put it inside in a closet or drawer.

5. Wait for one week.

6. Compare the coat hangers. What has happened to the rubber bands?

7. Explanation: the pollution outdoors should have cracked the rubber bands, while the rubber bands on the hanger that was indoors should still be fine. Depending on the level of pollution in your area, it may take longer than a week to see a change in the rubber bands.

ENVIRONMENT:
Match Game (B3)

Materials:

❑ Paper

❑ Writing instruments

Directions:

1. Have children search outside and try to create a list of the following in 30 minutes:
   - 10 insects
   - 10 birds
   - 10 animals
   - 10 trees
   - 10 plants

2. Kids can work individually or in groups.

3. At the end of 30 minutes, let groups share their lists in a round robin fashion. That means one group shares one item on their list, then another group goes, etc.

4. When a group shares an item on its list, it gets a point for every group that did NOT have that item on its list.

5. Round robin continues until everyone's list is exhausted.

Source: Adapted from Gayle Jo Carter's article "Dig Into Your Backyard" from *USA Weekend* of June 9-11, 2006.

ENVIRONMENT:
Adjective Scavenger Hunt (B4)

Materials:

- ❑ Egg cartons (1 per participant or group)
- ❑ Markers

Directions:

1. This is a nice twist on the traditional scavenger hunt.

2. Each participant gets an egg carton.

3. In each section of the egg carton, write an adjective or other descriptive word that can describe something in nature. Examples include soft, hard, spiky, smooth, blue, beautiful, old, fragile, yummy, closed, open, wet or dry.

4. Kids can help generate the list and write the words inside the egg cartons.

5. Kids can then work alone or in groups to see if they can fill all 12 sections of the egg carton.

Source: http://wilderdom.com/games/EnvironmentalActivities.html

ENVIRONMENT:
Field Guides (B5)

Materials:

- ❑ Camera
- ❑ Paper
- ❑ Writing instruments
- ❑ Notebook for assembling pages

- ❑ Glue
- ❑ Tape
- ❑ Scissors

Directions:

1. Children can create their own field guides of your program's grounds.

2. Take photos or make drawings of interesting animals, plants, or geological areas.

3. Write short descriptions of each.

4. Assemble photos and/or drawings into a book format for your program field guide.

5. Put out for families to see.

6. For another twist, see if kids who didn't assemble field guides can find where the pictures were taken.

Source: Adapted from Kathleen Carroll's *A Guide to Great Field Trips* (2007 Zephyr Press)

ENVIRONMENT:
Wet Noses (B6)

Materials:

❑ Water   ❑ Sponges

Directions:

1. Wet the underside of child's nose with a small wet sponge.

2. This improves their sense of smell just as it does for deer and rabbits..

3. Find familiar smells such as flowers to try, then go on to other things like rubbing a leaf between your fingers and smelling or scratching a pine needle.

4. Also try moss, bark, pitch or grabbing an handful of leafy soil etc.

Source: http://www.naturepark.com/act.htm

ENVIRONMENT:
Discover Color in Nature (B7)

Materials:

❑ Paint swatches ❑ Scissors

Directions:

1. Get 10 old paint swatches of various natural colors from a paint store.

2. Cut them into individual squares and take these and the kids to a natural area.

3. One at a time, have kids look for each color in nature.

4. You will be amazed at what colors you can find if you really look!

Source: http://www.naturepark.com/act.htm

ENVIRONMENT:
Touching Nature (B8)

Materials:

☐ Blindfold for each child

Directions:

1. Blindfold kids and lead them to a tree to get to know it by feeling the bark texture, finding branches and any other way to recognize a specific tree without looking at it.

2. Still blind-folded, lead your child back to where you started.

3. Now take off the blindfold and have them try to find their tree using their sense of touch to confirm it.

4. What other senses helped them to locate their tree? (sounds, sense of balance, smells, warmth etc.)

Source: http://www.naturepark.com/act.htm

ENVIRONMENT:
Mobiles (B9)

Materials:

- ❑ Various objects from nature
- ❑ Sticks roughly 1 foot in length (2 per child)
- ❑ String
- ❑ Glue
- ❑ Hot glue gun

Directions:

1. Kids can gather various materials from nature (rocks, twigs, leaves, shells, nuts, etc.).

2. The two sticks should be tied/glued together in an "X" shape.

3. Glue objects to strings. Adults will need to assist if a hot glue gun is necessary.

4. Tie strings to sticks. Encourage kids to think about how to balance their mobiles.

5. Let dry for about a day.

6. Hang mobiles!

ROCKS

ROCKS:
Rock Hunt (C1)

Materials:

❑ magnifying glasses

❑ books about different kinds of rocks

Directions:

1. Ideally, adult should have a variety of books about rocks.

2. While on the hike, children should collect different kinds of rocks.

3. Upon return to the room have children put rocks in a central location for everyone to see.

4. Have children group rocks by characteristics such as size, shape, color, and feel.

ROCKS:
Rock Displays (C2)

Materials:

- variety of rocks
- cardboard (box lids work best)
- glue
- markers
- books about different kinds of rocks

Directions:

1. This activity is intended to be a follow-up activity to the rock hunt.

2. After categorizing rocks, let children group them on cardboard as they see fit.

3. They can label them by their own categories and/ or try to identify them through books.

ROCKS:
I Spy with Rocks (C3)

Materials:

☐ variety of rocks

Directions:

1. One child is chosen to be "it" and secretly picks a rock.

2. Other children try to guess which rock it is by asking questions that can be answered with yes or no, such as, "is it smooth?" or "is it gray?"

3. When a child guesses correctly, (s)he may have a turn.

ROCKS:
Categories (C4)

Materials:

☐ variety of rocks

☐ egg shell cartons

Directions:

1. Kids can use rocks for sorting and making up their own games.

2. Kids can use egg shell cartons to sort rocks into various categories. Consider: size, color, texture (smooth, rough), etc.

3. You could also have kids go on a rock hunt and do a scavenger hunt to find rocks to fit each category that you select. Each child could be given half an egg carton with instructions to fill each hole with a certain kind of rock. First child to fill all the holes wins.

ROCKS:
Pet Rocks (C5)

Materials:

- [ ] rocks
- [ ] paint
- [ ] paintbrushes
- [ ] paint shirts
- [ ] newspaper
- [ ] small boxes (shoe boxes are ideal)
- [ ] construction paper
- [ ] scissors
- [ ] glue
- [ ] markers
- [ ] odds and ends (lids, spools, yarn, felt scraps, etc.)

Directions:

1. Let kids go on a rock hunt to find their perfect pet rocks.

2. Kids can then decorate rocks as they wish.

3. Finally, kids can use boxes and other materials to create houses for their pet rocks if they wish.

4. It could also be fun for them to create an instruction book for proper care and feeding for pet rocks.

ROCKS:
Rock Necklace (C6)

Materials:

- Rocks
- Markers or paint
- #20 hemp rope
- Scissors
- Low temp glue gun

Directions:

1. Kids can use especially attractive rocks or use markers or paints to decorate rocks.

2. Cut a piece of hemp rope about 1 yard.

3. Attach to the back of the rock with glue gun.

4. Wrap hemp around rock several times, securing with glue as necessary.

5. Tie ends together to form necklace, trimming rope if necessary.

6. A shell could be used instead of a rock as well.

Source: http://www.makingfriends.com/rocknecklace.htm

ROCKS:
A Pound of Rocks (C7)

Materials:

- Postal scale
- Bags
- Notebook to record observations
- Writing instruments

Directions:

1. Give kids a postal scale and ask them to weigh objects. Let them get a sense of how much a pound weighs.

2. Go outside and let kids gather rocks in bags. They can work individually or in groups.

3. The objective is for kids to try to gather enough rocks to equal a pound.

4. Once they've gathered their rocks, they can weigh them on the scale to see how close they got.

5. If desired, kids can record guesses in a notebook.

EARTH SCIENCE

EARTH SCIENCE:
Forming Sedimentary Rocks (D1)

Materials:

- ❑ plastic jars (2 liter bottles work best)
- ❑ plaster of Paris
- ❑ sand
- ❑ mud
- ❑ gravel
- ❑ shells
- ❑ water
- ❑ matte knife

Directions:

1. This activity will require discussion first about what sedimentary rocks are. Explain that the ground is made of millions of years of layered rock, sand, and soil. Having books on rocks available would also be helpful.

2. In the bottom of a plastic bottle, pour 1-2 inches of dry sand mixed with the same amount of dry plaster of Paris.

3. Add a layer of gravel and another layer of sand, both mixed with dry plaster of Paris.

4. Study the different layers and drop a few shells in while adding the different mixtures.

5. Add water until all areas are saturated.

6. Let it set for a couple of days.

7. When the layers have hardened, split the plastic jar open and study each layer. You can also split the layers apart to find the hidden shells.

EARTH SCIENCE:
Hidden Treasures (D2)

Materials:

- ❑ assorted rocks, shells, fossils, bones, etc.
- ❑ individual paper bowls
- ❑ plaster of Paris
- ❑ water
- ❑ paper

Directions:

1. Gather materials to be buried in the plaster.

2. Trace each object on a piece of paper. This will create a map to go by when digging later.

3. Mix plaster of Paris and pour over objects.

4. Hide objects a layer at a time.

EARTH SCIENCE:
Archeology Dig in Plaster (D3)

Materials:

- hidden treasures from D2 activity
- map from D2 activity
- tools for digging such as metal forks
- stiff brushes
- dust masks
- newspaper

Directions:

1. This is messy, so is best done outside or over newspaper.

2. This activity may also take several days to complete.

3. Once plaster has hardened from hidden treasures activity, kids can now dig up the objects.

4. As each object is found, it can be placed on the map.

EARTH SCIENCE:
Dig Up Your Backyard (D4)

Materials:

- Shovels
- Pails
- Trowels
- Magnifying glass

- Notebooks/paper
- Graph paper
- Writing instruments
- Sandwich bags

Directions:

1. Make sure you check this out with whoever is in charge of your program's building first!

2. Dig a 2' x 2' x 2' section in the ground.

3. Children can note every item they find - rocks, wood chips, sticks, etc.

4. Pinpoint items on graph paper and label and place them in individual bags for collection.

5. Don't forget to refill hole with dirt when you're finished!

Source: Gayle Jo Carter's article "Dig Into Your Backyard" from *USA Weekend* of June 9-11, 2006.

EARTH SCIENCE:
The Disappearing Chicken Bone
(D5)

❑ Shovel   ❑ Chicken bone

Directions:

1. Dig a hole, roughly a foot deep.

2. Bury a chicken bone in the hole.

3. Dig the bone up again in two weeks.

4. Compare it to a fresh chicken bone.

5. Ask the kids to imagine what a bone would look like after it had been in the ground for a week, a month, a year, 5000 years.

6. Kids could also rebury the bone and check on it again after a predetermined time.

Source: Gayle Jo Carter's article "Dig Into Your Backyard" from *USA Weekend* of June 9-11, 2006.

EARTH SCIENCE:
Preserving Fossils (D6)

Materials:

- [ ] paper plate
- [ ] paper cup
- [ ] sea shell or other textured objects

- [ ] modeling clay
- [ ] petroleum jelly
- [ ] plaster of Paris
- [ ] plastic spoon

Directions:

1. Place a piece of clay about the size of a lemon on a paper plate.
2. Rub petroleum jelly on the outside of the sea shell.
3. Press the shell into the clay.
4. Mix four spoons of plaster with two spoons of water in the paper cup.
5. Pour the mixture into the shell imprint in the clay.
6. Throw the cup and spoon away.
7. Let the plaster harden. It will take 15-20 minutes.
8. Separate the clay and the plaster mold. You should now have your very own fossil!

EARTH SCIENCE:
Insect Fossils (D7)

Materials:

- ❑ Clear nail polish
- ❑ Small dead insect or plastic insect model
- ❑ Bottle cap
- ❑ Pine cones (optional)

Directions:

1. Place insect in small bottle cap.

2. Slowly drip clear nail polish over insect.

3. Let it dry and repeat the process.

4. Over time, the insect will be completely encased in the hardened nail polish, just like a true amber fossil.

Source: http://www.seedsofknowledge.com/dinosaurs.html

EARTH SCIENCE:
Building a Volcano (D8)

Materials:

- book on volcanoes
- mud
- dirt
- twigs
- jar or glass
- possibly a small lamp shade as frame for volcano
- paint shirts

Directions:

1. Discuss volcanoes - how they work, where they can be found, etc.
2. This project is best outside.
3. Use a strong board or sturdy, shallow box to hold volcano in.
4. Children should work in groups to build their own volcano.
5. They must leave a spot at the top to insert the jar.
6. Volcano will need to dry overnight.

EARTH SCIENCE:
Erupting a Volcano (D9)

Materials:

- Volcano from D7 activity
- jar or glass
- heavy board or box
- spoon
- baking soda
- water
- liquid detergent
- vinegar
- red food coloring

Directions:

1. Place jar in top of volcano.

2. Put 3 or 4 spoonfuls of baking soda in jar.

3. Mix the following separately:
   - 1/2 cup water
   - 1/4 cup detergent
   - 1/4 cup vinegar
   - red food coloring

4. Pour the mixture in the jar and watch what happens!

5. Let kids then experiment with adding more or less of certain ingredients or leaving some out and seeing what happens.

LEAVES & TREES

LEAVES & TREES:
Leaf Hike (E1)

Materials:

❑ none

Directions:

1. Ideally, adult should have a variety of library books about leaves and flowers.

2. Before going on the hike be sure children can identify poison ivy, oak, etc.

3. While on the hike, children should collect different kinds of leaves and flowers.

4. Upon return to the room have children put leaves and flowers in a central location for everyone to see.

5. Have children group leaves by characteristics such as size, shape, color, edges, feel, smell, and veins.

LEAVES & TREES:
I Spy with Leaves (E2)

Materials:

❑ variety of leaves

Directions:

1. One child is chosen to be "it" and secretly picks a leaf.

2. Other children try to guess which leaf it is by asking yes/no questions such as, "does it have wavy edges?" or "do the veins branch out?"

3. When a child guesses correctly, (s)he may have a turn.

LEAVES & TREES:
Categories (E3)

Materials:

❑ variety of leaves

Directions:

1. Kids can use leaves for sorting and making up their own games.

2. Consider: size, shape, color, texture (smooth, rough), etc.

3. You could also have kids go on a leaf hunt and do a scavenger hunt to find leaves to fit each category that you select.

LEAVES & TREES:
Leaf Rainbow (E4)

Materials:

☐ Bags (1 per person)
☐ Variety of leaves

☐ Construction paper
☐ Glue

Directions:

1. Kids go on a walk and collect leaves.

2. Kids can then group their leaves by color and glue them to paper to make a rainbow.

3. You may choose to make one large rainbow as an entire group and then let kids make their own individual pictures.

4. Kids may also choose to make collages or other pictures with the leaves.

5. Encourage kids to try to make pictures with only the leaves and without cutting them.

Source: Adapted from
http://wilderdom.com/games/EnvironmentalActivities.html

LEAVES & TREES:
Leaf Rubbings (E5)

Materials:

☐ leaves   ☐ crayons

☐ paper

Directions:

1. Place leaves underneath the paper and rub the side of a crayon over the paper.

2. Discuss the different textures of the leaves.

3. Consider cutting out the leaves to make a wall mural or tree bulletin board.

4. This activity could also be done with various other objects collected in or outdoors.

LEAVES & TREES:
Leaf Pressings (E6)

Materials:

- [ ] variety of leaves
- [ ] newspaper
- [ ] heavy books
- [ ] glue
- [ ] cellophane wrap
- [ ] poster board

Directions:

1. Collect a leaf or two from a specific tree. The leaves should be as free from holes and tears as possible. It is better (for the tree anyway) if you can find good leaves that have fallen from the tree.

2. Lay leaves on newspaper and cover with more newspaper.

3. Stack heavy books or other weight on top of newspaper.

4. The newspaper should be changed every few days until leaves are dry.

5. Once dry leaves can be glued onto poster board, covered with cellophane, and labeled.

6. Stems and flowers can also be pressed. Those that aren't too thick will work best.

7. This should take a day or two, depending on the thickness of the leaf.

LEAVES & TREES:
Leaf Prints (E7)

Materials:

- Pressed leaves (see E5 activity)
- Newspaper
- Heavy books or other weight
- Colored ink
- Small dish
- Old toothbrush
- Short stick
- Fine mesh screen

Directions:

1. Cover table with newspapers.

2. Pour some ink into dish, and dip an old toothbrush into the ink.

3. Practice making spatters by scraping a short stick toward you (not away) through the bristles. This causes the ink to spatter away from you. You can also run the toothbrush over a fine mesh screen held over the leaf.

4. Practice until you can get a fine, controlled spatter. Place the leaf onto a piece of art paper and spatter around the edges of pressed leaves.

Source: http://bizarrelabs.com/plant2.htm

LEAVES & TREES:
Preserving Leaves (E8)

Materials:

- ❑ Variety of fresh leaves picked from tree
- ❑ Water
- ❑ Glycerin (readily available in many pharmacies)
- ❑ Pan

Directions:

1. Some leaves, such as holly, magnolia, and some maples, can be preserved by using glycerin. By trial and error you can determine which types of leaves work best by this method. You can capture fall colors in leaves fairly well using this method. Pick the leaves just as they are turning.

2. Add 2 parts boiling water to 1 part glycerin.

3. Place leaf in the warm glycerin solution so that stem is submerged 3-4 inches.

4. How long the process takes depends on the type of leaf, but you will know enough has been absorbed when drops of glycerin appear on the surface of the leaf.

5. Remove leaf from solution and wipe to remove excess.

6. Drain on thick stacks of newspaper for a few days, then wash (not too rough!) with a little soap and water. Hang on a line (wooden clothespins are useful here) to dry.

Source: http://bizarrelabs.com/plant2.htm

LEAVES & TREES:
Match Game (E9)

Materials:

- ☐ Bags
- ☐ Leaves
- ☐ Twigs
- ☐ Nuts
- ☐ Notepads
- ☐ Pencils/pens
- ☐ String
- ☐ Tape measures

Directions:

1. This is a game in which the object is to find clues and describe a tree well enough that someone else can find it.

2. Half of the group goes outside. Each person finds his or her own tree.

3. The child can gather clues in his/her bag from the tree (leaves, twigs, nuts, bark, etc.)

4. The child can also write down observations about the tree (where it is, how wide around it is by measuring with a string or tape measure, how tall it is - see E10, etc.)

5. After each child has gathered enough clues and information, the group goes back in.

6. Each child who was outside is now partnered with someone who was inside.

7. The inside group now goes outdoors and tries to find his/her partner's tree based on the clues.

LEAVES & TREES:
Measuring the Height of a Tree (E10)

Materials:

❑ Tape measure   ❑ Yardstick

Directions:

1. Use the tape measure to measure off exactly 25 feet from the tree you wish to measure.

2. With the zero end of the yardstick downward, hold the yardstick exactly 25 inches from your eye.

3. Line up the bottom of the yardstick with the base of the tree.

4. Note which inch line marks the top of the tree. Each inch equals one foot of the tree's height.

5. If the tree is taller than the yardstick, stand 50 feet away from tree. Follow steps 2-4 again, but this time double the final number. If still taller, than back away 75 feet, follow steps 2-4, and triple the number. For 100 feet, 4x the number, etc.

Source: http://bizarrelabs.com/tree.htm

LEAVES & TREES:
Chlorophyll and Autumn Colors
(E11)

Materials:

- Plant (geraniums work well for this)
- Black paper
- Paper clip or tape
- Alcohol
- Iodine solution
- Cups

Directions:

1. Cover half of a leaf (still attached to the plant) with black paper.

2. Put the plant in sunlight for 48 hours.

3. Remove the black paper and one half of the leaf should be yellow-ish.

4. Chlorophyll, which is what makes a plant green, will break down if it does not receive sunlight for an extended period of time. The base color of many leaves is yellow, which is why some leaves turn yellow in the autumn; the other fall colors are due to chemical changes within the leaves.

5. Remove the leaf from the plant and soak it in warm alcohol until the chlorophyll has been removed from it. If the leaf is now dipped in iodine solution, the part that has received sunlight will turn blue, as iodine turns blue in the presence of starch.

Source: http://bizarrelabs.com/plant1.htm

PLANTS & SEEDS

PLANTS & SEEDS:
What Makes Them Grow? (F1)

Materials:

❑ None

Directions:

1. Tell kids you are going on an adventure to find out what makes plants grow.

2. Take kids outside and ask them to make notes about where they see the most plants growing.

3. Why are plants growing in some places and not others?

4. The kids' observations of what makes plants grow or not grow in certain areas may include the amount of sunlight, water, dirt, and erosion.

5. They might also discuss how some areas are highly trafficked and won't allow for much growth and how other areas (such as a tended garden) that are specifically taken care of to allow for plant growth.

PLANTS & SEEDS:
Weeds (F2)

Materials:

- ❑ Plant/weed guide book
- ❑ Small bags
- ❑ Paper
- ❑ Writing and drawing instruments
- ❑ Crayons without paper for rubbings

Directions:

1. Find weeds growing around your program area.

2. Collect them to bring inside and compare.

3. Check your local library for plant guides to see if you can identify the different weeds.

4. See if you can find out how different weeds may be useful. For example, dandelions were brought to the United States from Europe for salads, soups, and as a coffee substitute.

5. Children can also draw the different weeds or try to do rubbings with them.

Source: Adapted from Kathleen Carroll's *A Guide to Great Field Trips* (2007 Zephyr Press)

PLANTS & SEEDS:
Greenhouse in a Bag (F3)

Materials:

- ❑ sealable plastic bags
- ❑ paper towels
- ❑ large, quick sprouting seeds (radish, peas, or beans work well)

Directions:

1. Place a damp paper towel in each bag.

2. Put some seeds in each bag and label them with kind of seed and child's name.

3. Arrange on a shelf or in shallow boxes so that they can be observed.

4. If bags are locked shut, the toweling will stay moist and the seeds will grow in about 3 weeks.

5. If it should dry up, add a bit of water.

PLANTS & SEEDS:
Milk Carton Gardens (F4)

Materials:

- ❑ variety of seeds
- ❑ milk cartons or egg cartons
- ❑ potting soil
- ❑ spoons
- ❑ water
- ❑ water can or cups

Directions:

1. This activity can be done in or outdoors. If done inside, use plenty of newspaper underneath.

2. Discuss different types of seeds. See if children can guess what grows from each kind.

3. Let children choose which kind of seed they would like to plant.

4. Put small holes in the bottom of the cartons.

5. Children should label their carton.

6. Fill the cartons with potting soil and then plant the seeds.

7. Water and place in a sunny spot.

8. Observe the seeds over the summer and discuss any changes that may occur.

9. Don't forget to water periodically!

PLANTS & SEEDS:
Fruits and Vegetables (F5)

Materials:

- Variety of fruit and vegetable seeds (oranges, grapefruits, apples, lemons, tomatoes)
- Small pots
- Good garden soil
- Avocado pits
- Toothpicks
- Glass jars
- Water
- Potato and sweet potato cuttings
- Carrot tops

Directions:

1. Plant seeds in pots with soil, about twice as deep as they are wide.

2. Stick toothpicks in avocado pits to support them on top of a glass filled with water. The wide end of the seed should be just submerged in the water. Keep glass filled with water.

3. For potatoes and sweet potatoes, make sure cutting has at least one "eye", which is where the potato vine will grow. The eye needs to be out of the water.

4. Carrot tops will also grow this way if the root end is kept submerged.

5. All of these must be transplanted to soil eventually; water alone won't keep plant growing.

Source: http://bizarrelabs.com/plant1.htm

PLANTS & SEEDS:
Powerful Seeds (F6)

Materials:

- ❑ clear plastic cups
- ❑ plaster of Paris
- ❑ water
- ❑ lima bean seeds
- ❑ potting soil

Directions:

1. Fill two clear plastic cups half full of potting soil.

2. Place three lima bean seeds on top of the soil in both cups.

3. Add water to moisten the soil; do not soak it.

4. Mix plaster of Paris, a little more watery than usual. It should be runny.

5. Pour a thin layer over the beans in one cup - just enough to cover the soil.

6. Record predictions from the kids about what will happen.

7. Watch over the next 2 weeks.

PLANTS & SEEDS:
What Shape Is Grass? (F7)

Materials:

- Cookie cutters
- New sponge
- Grass seed
- Plant mister
- Plastic wrap
- Cookie sheets
- Colored markers

Directions:

1. Before hand, staff should rinse sponges well to remove pretreated disinfectants. Then let dry.

2. Trace around cookie cutter on to sponge.

3. Cut out shape traced on to the sponge.

4. Dampen sponge lightly and then put back inside cookie cutter.

5. Sprinkle grass seed on sponge and then spray with plant mister and cover with plastic wrap.

6. Place shapes on cookie sheet so dampness won't seep through.

7. Remove plastic wrap when shoots appear and spray with plant mister daily.

Source: http://familyfun.go.com

PLANTS & SEEDS:
Green-Haired Monster (F8)

Materials:

- ❑ Newspaper
- ❑ Potting soil
- ❑ Grass seed
- ❑ Small stones

- ❑ Construction paper
- ❑ Markers or crayons
- ❑ Planter for each child (preferably recyclables)

Directions:

1. Spread newspaper over work surface.

2. Children can cut out construction paper to fit around the container.

3. Then kids can design their favorite monster faces on the paper and glue it to the containers.

4. Fill each container with potting soil. Put small stones in the bottom of container to improve drainage.

5. Add grass seed on top.

6. Water until damp, not soaked.

7. Water a little each day and make sure they get plenty of sun.

8. Kids can give their monsters "haircuts" as the grass grows.

Source: www.childrenshungeralliance.org

PLANTS & SEEDS:
There's Something Growing on Your Sock (F9)

- ❏ Old fuzzy athletic sock (1 per child)
- ❏ Flower pots and/or shoe boxes
- ❏ Plastic garbage bags or plastic wrap
- ❏ Soil
- ❏ Scissors

Directions:

1. Each child pulls a sock over his/her shoe and head out for a nature walk.

2. Be sure you walk across a variety of surfaces so that kids' socks will pick up lots of different stuff.

3. After walk, kids remove socks.

4. Each child gets a flower pot or shoe box lined with a plastic garbage bag or plastic wrap.

5. Cut a slit down the side of each sock and flatten the sock.

6. Plant it with the seeds pointing up. Cover the sock with a thin layer of soil.

7. Place plants in a sunny window and water daily.

8. Within a week or two, kids should start seeing what mystery plants have sprouted from the socks.

Source: http://pbskids.org/zoom/activities/sci/sockseeds.html

PLANTS & SEEDS:
Pop Bottle Terrarium (F10)

Materials:

- plastic 2-liter pop bottle with cap
- potting soil
- small plant(s) that require little watering
- duct tape
- water

Directions:

1. Cut the bottom from the plastic bottle (about 3 1/2").

2. Put soil in the piece you've just cut and place your small plant in the soil.

3. Cover the roots, press the soil firmly and add a little water.

4. Fit the bottle over the base and secure with duct tape.

5. Make sure you put terrarium where plant will get proper lighting.

PLANTS & SEEDS:
Moss Terrarium (F11)

Materials:

- ☐ Moss
- ☐ Plastic sandwich bags
- ☐ Water
- ☐ Large, clean glass jar with tight-fitting lid
- ☐ Shallow box
- ☐ Sand and pebbles
- ☐ Soil from same place as moss (or a mix of charcoal, light gravel, leaf mold, and garden soil)

Directions:

1. Collect moss in bags. Sprinkle with water and seal bag if you aren't setting up terrarium right away.

2. Lay jar on its side in box so that it will not roll.

3. Place sand and pebbles about an inch thick in the bottom of the jar.

4. Now fill with soil to the level of the opening of the jar. A little sulfur scattered on the soil will help prevent mold.

5. Plant the moss by pressing it into the soil.

6. Water terrarium, screw lid on, and place in shady place. If too wet, leave lid off a few hours to allow some water vapor to escape. Once you get the balance just right, the moss should thrive. The terrarium should sustain itself for weeks or months without more water if the lid is kept tightly on. You may even get stalks that will grow into new plants.

Source: http://bizarrelabs.com/plant1.htm

FLOWER & PLANT ART

FLOWER & PLANT ART:
Bleaching Flowers (G1)

Materials:

- ❑ Different colored flowers
- ❑ Ammonia
- ❑ Large jar
- ❑ Plastic lid that fits jar
- ❑ String

Directions:

1. Tie several different colored flowers together at the stems.

2. Place a little ammonia in the bottom of a large jar.

3. Tie flowers to string.

4. Hang flowers in jar so that they don't touch ammonia.

5. Secure lid to hold the string in place.

6. In a few minutes, the colors will fade from some of the flowers, especially any reds, purples, or pinks (not so much with white or yellow). The petals of some of the flowers will appear greenish due to the chlorophyll within.

Source: http://bizarrelabs.com/plant1.htm

FLOWER & PLANT ART:
Drying Flowers (G2)

Materials:

- ❑ Flowers (sturdy ones work best)
- ❑ Borax or white sand
- ❑ Knife for cutting (adult should do)
- ❑ Small cardboard box

Directions:

1. To preserve the shape of flowers, pour an inch or so of borax into the bottom of box.

2. Set the cut flowers, stem side down, into the borax.

3. Slowly and carefully cover the flowers with more borax.

4. Set the box in a sunny place for 2 or 3 weeks (delicate flowers dry faster - a week or so).

5. Carefully pour off the borax and save for the next drying.

6. The flowers will be fragile, but the shape and much of the color should be preserved.

Source: http://bizarrelabs.com/plant2.htm

FLOWER & PLANT ART:
Pressed Flower Placemats (G3)

Materials:

- ❑ Pressed flowers/leaves
- ❑ Clear contact paper
- ❑ Construction paper
- ❑ Scissors

Directions:

1. Cut two pieces of contact paper, approximately 9" x 12".

2. Before peeling backing paper off, kids can arrange flowers and leaves to get a sense of where they want them on the paper.

3. Peel the backing off one piece of contact paper and lay it sticky-side up on the table.

4. Arrange flowers and leaves on the sticky side of the contact paper.

5. If desired, cut a piece of construction paper the same size as the contact paper and lay it down over the flowers and leaves. Do this carefully to avoid bubbling.

6. Now peel the backing paper off the other piece of contact paper and stick it to the other side of the paper.

7. Use scissors to trim any uneven edges.

Source: http://fun.familyeducation.com/decorative-arts/childrens-art-activities/29576.html?detoured=1

FLOWER & PLANT ART:
Glowing Flowers (G4)

Materials:

- ❑ Pressed flowers or leaves
- ❑ Votive cup
- ❑ Tissue paper
- ❑ Decoupage solution
- ❑ Foam brushes

Directions:

1. Tear off the straight edges from a sheet of tissue paper. Then tear the tissue paper into small pieces.

2. Brush the outside of the votive cup with decoupage solution.

3. Arrange pressed flowers or leaves all around the glass.

4. Brush on more glue.

5. Lay the pieces of paper on the glass, overlapping the edges.

6. Keep adding paper and glue until the entire glass is covered.

Source: http://www.makingfriends.com/votive_flowers.htm

FLOWER & PLANT ART:
Fabric Prints (G5)

Materials:

- Fresh leaves or flowers
- Unbleached muslin or other fabric
- Old newspapers or cardboard
- Rubber mallet, hammer, or wooden blocks
- Heavy paper or card stock

Directions:

1. Put old newspaper or cardboard on hard work surface.
2. Cut fabric to desired size.
3. Place fabric on work surface.
4. Place one leaf/flower anywhere on the material.
5. Use the hammer/mallet/wood blocks to pound on the entire leaf.
6. Continue placing leaves on material and hammer each completely.
7. You may choose to place a new leaf/flower over an already pounded leaf for more color.

Source: http://www.flower-press.com/leaf-pounding.htm

FLOWER & PLANT ART:
Twig Vase (G6)

Materials:

- ❑ Twigs
- ❑ Rubber bands
- ❑ Empty jar
- ❑ Twine or ribbon
- ❑ Glue

Directions:

1. Break twigs so that they are an inch longer than the height of the jar.

2. Wrap a rubber band around the neck of the jar, about an inch from the top.

3. Wrap another band around the jar, about an inch from the bottom.

4. Place the twigs around the jar, tucking the ends under the rubber bands.

5. When the jar is covered with twigs, slide the rubber bands toward each other, so that they meet in the middle of the jar.

6. Take a few pieces of twine or ribbon and wrap them around the rubber bands.

7. To finish off the vase, you can make a bow with ribbon or simply glue the ends in place.

Source: http://fun.familyeducation.com/decorative-arts/childrens-art-activities/29574.html?detoured=1

FLOWER & PLANT ART:
Twig Easel (G7)

Materials:

- [ ] Twigs
- [ ] Garden clippers
- [ ] Hot glue gun
- [ ] Twine or yarn

- [ ] Scissors
- [ ] Small piece of cardboard
- [ ] Crayons, markers, or paint

Directions:

1. An adult should cut three long twigs and one short one.

2. The adult then hot glues to attach the twigs together, forming an A shape with the short stick as the line that goes across.

3. Wrap the joints with twine or yarn.

4. Glue the last twig to where the other two long twigs meet, forming a tripod. Wrap it with twine.

5. Cut a piece of cardboard to fit on the easel. Paint or draw a picture on the cardboard.

6. Now cut four twigs to size and hot glue them around the edges of the cardboard to form a frame.

7. Rest the framed cardboard picture on the easel.

Source: http://www.zoomwhales.com/crafts/twigs/twigeasel/

FLOWER & PLANT ART:
Potpourri Pinecones (G8)

Materials:

- Pinecones
- Newpaper
- Water
- Glue
- Cinnamon cloves and other spices
- Plastic bowls (1 per spice)
- Paintbrush
- Mixing bowl
- Spoon
- Small basket or decorative bowl

Directions:

1. Cover work area with newspaper.
2. In mixing bowl, mix ½ cup of glue with a ½ cup of water.
3. Put each spice in a separate plastic bowl.
4. Use the paintbrush to cover an entire pinecone with the glue mixture.
5. Roll the pinecone in the spices. Cover the entire pinecone.
6. Set pinecones aside to dry for a few hours.
7. Display several in a small basket or decorative bowl.

Source: http://fun.familyeducation.com/decorative-arts/childrens-art-activities/29571.html?detoured=1

HABITATS

HABITATS:
A Small Plot of Land (H1)

Materials:

- ❏ String
- ❏ Sticks
- ❏ Chalk
- ❏ Yardstick

- ❏ Paper
- ❏ Writing utensils
- ❏ Small paper bags

Directions:

1. Even on a school playground, kids may be surprised how much they observe if they get down on their hands and knees and pay attention to the ground.

2. You can even measure off actual plots for kids and mark them with string tied to sticks to designate their spots. Use chalk on playground surfaces.

3. You can decide with kids how big the plot is, but even a few square feet will work fine.

4. The object is for kids to see how much they can observe about nature on just their small plot of land. What kinds of plants and weeds do they see? What kinds of insects? Are there any sticks, leaves, nuts, rocks, or seeds? How many different kinds of any of these items do they see?

5. You can also provide kids with paper and writing utensils to draw or write about what they observe.

6. Finally, you might want to have kids collect materials on their plot of land for a future project, such as a collage.

HABITATS:
Ocean in a Bottle (H2)

Materials:

- ❑ Empty two liter plastic bottle with lid
- ❑ Clear vegetable oil or mineral oil
- ❑ Water funnel
- ❑ Food coloring
- ❑ Glitter
- ❑ Small star fish, shells and other sea creatures (can find at local craft or discount store)
- ❑ White craft glue
- ❑ Hot glue

Directions:

1. Wash and dry bottle and remove all labels.

2. Fill bottle halfway with tap water. Add a few drops of food coloring and swirl around to mix.

3. Add glitter and sea creatures. Use lightweight starfish, shells and other sea creature toys that float.

4. Using a funnel, fill the rest of the bottle with vegetable oil.

5. Be sure that rim and cap are dry, then apply white craft glue around the rim.

6. Seal cap. Use a layer of hot glue around the outer edge of the cap for added protection from leakage.

7. Turn bottle on its side and gently rock the bottle to create a "wave" inside your ocean habitat!

Source: http://crafts.kaboose.com/ocean-in-a-bottle.html

HABITATS:
Bug Cages (H3)

Materials:

- two large jar lids that are the same size
- window screen
- plaster of Paris
- ruler
- scissors

Directions:

1. Measure the circumference of a jar lid with string, allowing 2 cm. to overlap.

2. Cut the string and use to measure a length of window screen. Mark length with a marker.

3. Use a ruler to draw a line perpendicular to the measured edge. Draw a straight line for the top of the rectangle. A good ratio is 1 (height) to 1/2 (length). Cages that are too tall tend to sag and tilt.

4. Roll the screen and overlap the sides.

5. Hold onto the tube and put the lids on both ends to check for fit.

6. To secure the screen, take one lid off and staple the length of the seam several times.

7. Replace the lid and repeat for the other end.

8. Pour plaster of Paris into one lid. This seals the screen to the lid and creates the base. The top lid should be tight, but removable. Let the plaster harden overnight before adding creatures.

HABITATS:
Butterfly Feeder (H4)

Materials:

- Small jar (such as a baby food or jelly jar) with a lid
- Sugar
- Water
- Cotton
- Materials for decorating feeders (if desired)
- Means for hanging feeder

Directions:

1. Make a small hole in the lid of the jar.

2. Make butterfly food by dissolving one part sugar in nine parts of water.

3. Fill the jar with butterfly food.

4. Screw the lid tightly onto the jar and poke a small piece of cotton into the hole.

5. Decorate jars with paint or decoupage. Butterflies locate their food sources by sight, so the more the feeder looks like a plant or flower, the better the chance of attracting butterflies. It may also help to cut out some fabric or plastic 'petals' and fasten them to the lid of your feeder.

6. Invert the jar and hang it in the garden.

Source: http://www.seedsofknowledge.com/butterflies2.html

HABITATS:
Butterfly Garden (H5)

Materials:

- Plot for garden
- Various plants, based on directions below
- Small shovels
- Trowels
- Planting soil

Directions:

1. **The Plot:** Butterflies thrive in a plot that receives 6 hours of sunlight each day. A site sheltered from the wind by trees, shrubs, or a building, will keep tall plants from blowing over, and allow your butterflies to feed, mate, and lay eggs in relative tranquility. Plant diversity will attract a variety of butterflies.

2. **Nectar flowers:** These flowers provide the food for butterflies. Nectar plants include butterfly weed, lantana, butterfly bush, black eyed Susan, purple coneflower, lavender, cosmos, zinnia, and marigold. Butterflies are attracted to masses of color and fragrance, so try to plant groups of flowers instead of single plants.

3. **Food for the Larvae:** Primary plants for butterfly larvae include aspen, alfalfa, clover, nettle, pearly everlasting, milkweed, grasses, hackberry, parsley, vetch, and willow.

4. The website also recommends providing puddles, overwintering sites for butterflies and pupae, and dark stones where butterflies can bask in the sun. The website also recommends using only nature friendly pest control..

Source:
http://www.kidsgardening.com/Dig/DigDetail.taf?ID=1667&Type=Art

HABITATS:
Habitat Diorama (H6)

Materials:

- ❑ shoe boxes
- ❑ construction paper
- ❑ glue
- ❑ scissors

- ❑ junk art
- ❑ markers
- ❑ crayons
- ❑ chalk

Directions:

1. Kids can go on a nature hike to collect items for their dioramas.

2. Upon return from the hike discuss ideas for different animal habitats such as a forest, desert, or a stream bed.

3. Each child can create a display of a specific habitat with the shoe box.

HABITATS:
Cycle Tank Construction (H7)

Materials:

- ❑ covered glass or plastic terrarium
- ❑ gravel and pebbles
- ❑ soil with living organisms
- ❑ small log, leaves, etc.

Directions:

1. Begin with any covered glass or plastic terrarium no smaller than 30 cm x 15 cm.

2. A cover such as a screen or clear plastic wrap is necessary to contain the insects.

3. Be sure there are holes for air to circulate.

4. Materials for the inside layer can be found outside.

5. The bottom layer should consist of roughly 3 cm of gravel and pebbles to help drainage.

6. The next layer should be soil. Confirm where it would okay to dig.

7. Add about 8 cm of soil with animals such as worms, bugs, and beetles.

8. On the top layer, place a small log, a few leaves, and anything else that looks interesting.

9. Keep and observe!

HABITATS:
Ant Farm (H8)

Materials:

- Large bottle or small aquarium
- Smaller bottle to fit inside first one
- Garden soil
- Funnel or paper cone
- Construction paper
- Scotch tape
- Garden shovel
- Bucket
- Cotton ball
- Honey
- Ants

Directions:

1. Place smaller container inside the larger one. Their should be about 1" of space between the two.

2. Find an ant farm and carefully dig where you see the most ants. Transfer soil, with the ants, into bucket. Try to find large, black ants (as these will be easiest to see) and, ideally, a queen ant with wings along with eggs and larvae.

3. Use the funnel/cone to gently pour the sand and worker ants into the space between the bottles.

4. Add the queen, eggs, and larvae last, sliding them gently down the funnel to rest on the soil.

5. Once ants are in place, put lid on container. Lay bottle on side and cover with dark paper to simulate underground.

6. You can add a drop of honey or sugar for food and a cotton ball soaked in water every couple days.

Source: http://www.allfreecrafts.com/nature/ant-farm.shtml

HABITATS:
Pine Cone Bird Feeders (H9)

Materials:

- ❑ peanut butter
- ❑ pine cones
- ❑ string

- ❑ birdseed
- ❑ butter knives

Directions:

1. Check for pine trees outside beforehand. If none are around, the adult will need to bring pine cones.

2. This is messy, so it is best done outside.

3. Let children pick out a pine cone.

4. Spread peanut butter all over the pine cone.

5. Sprinkle birdseed on the peanut butter.

6. Tie a string to the top of the pine cone to hang from a tree branch or outside overhang.

HABITATS:
Milk Jug Bird Feeders (H10)

Materials:

- plastic milk cartons - large
- birdseed
- construction paper
- markers
- crayons
- scissors
- glue
- string
- hole punch

Directions:

1. Children will cut a rectangular section out of one side of the milk carton.

2. Leave at least 2 inches of the plastic around the bottom.

3. Children may need help cutting into side of milk carton.

4. Ask the children what they could do to help the feeder blend into its surroundings.

5. After decorating, children punch holes in top of feeder and tie string through hole.

6. It may now be attached to a tree branch or other outside overhang.

7. Fill with birdseed.

HABITATS:
Paper Mache Bird Houses (H11)

Materials:

- Smocks
- Newspaper
- Water
- Flour
- Large pot

- Clean medium-sized milk carton
- Masking tape
- Scissors

Directions:

1. Tear newspaper into shreds and place in pot. Fill with water and boil for 30 minutes until paper turns to pulp.

2. Cool the pulp and squeeze out the water. Add 2 cups of flour and mix well.

3. Seal the top of the carton with masking tape and cut a hole larger than desired for finished product.

4. Cover whole carton (make sure pulp is on inside of hole as well) with paper mache pulp and leave to dry in sun.

5. When dry, add second layer and any desired decorations. Whole process may take a couple days.

6. Paint and add a coat of varnish for protection from the elements if desired.

Source: Adapted from http://www.kidzworld.com/

ANIMALS

ANIMALS:
Bug Hunt (I1)

Materials:

- ❏ bug container or wide mouth jar with lid (or bug cages from G3 activity)
- ❏ hammer
- ❏ large nail
- ❏ magnifying glass
- ❏ insect books

Directions:

1. Beforehand, the teacher should get several insect books from the library.

2. Discuss with the children what kinds of bugs they can find outside.

3. Kids may need to divide into groups to share bug containers.

4. While on the hike, children should collect different kinds of bugs.

5. Upon return, the kids should observe the bugs to see different characteristics. (antennas, number of legs, eyes, wings, color, protective coverings, etc.)

6. Without taking them out of their containers, have children group bugs by characteristics.

ANIMALS:
Insects and Temperature (I2)

Materials:

- several flies
- other insects (grasshoppers, ants, crickets)
- glass jar with lid
- shallow bowl
- thermometer
- thread
- crushed ice
- water

Directions:

1. Place several captured flies and other insects in a glass jar fitted with a lid with air holes.

2. Use a piece of thread to hang a thermometer inside the jar.

3. Hang the thread outside the jar and place the lid on tight. This should secure thermometer.

4. Observe the activity of all insects in the jar.

5. Read and record the temperature of the inside of the jar. Put the jar in a shallow bowl.

6. Pour a small amount of water into the bowl and add crushed ice around the jar.

7. Observe the insects. Note any changes and record temperature again.

8. When the insects have stopped moving and a last temp is recorded, remove the jar from the ice water.

9. When back to room temp, the insects will regain their activity.

ANIMALS:
Meal Worms (I3)

Materials:

- meal worms
- cornmeal or oatmeal
- plastic containers with lids
- magnifying glass

- toothpicks
- rulers
- paper towels or plates

Directions:

1. Pet stores sell meal worms in large quantities. They can make great cycle tank exhibits, but for observing, they work better in smaller containers with cornmeal or oatmeal.

2. In a matter of weeks, they will change from worm to pupa to grain beetle.

3. Each student should have a few worms on a paper towel or plate to observe.

4. Spend time observing meal worms with magnifying glasses, toothpicks, and rulers.

5. Discuss size, feel, color, smell, and physical features such as eyes, mouth, ears, antennae, and legs.

6. Use ruler to measure how far worm can travel in a minute.

7. Test to see if meal worms prefer light or dark surfaces.

8. See what they prefer to eat (sugar, bread, etc.). How do the worms react to milk? Vinegar? Water?

9. Record predictions and observations.

ANIMALS:
Ants (I4)

Materials:

- ☐ non-stinging ants
- ☐ sealable plastic bags
- ☐ spoons

- ☐ magnifying glass
- ☐ paper
- ☐ pencils

Directions:

1. It is a good idea to have resource books available. Suggested books include Cynthia Overbeck's *The World of Ants*, Arthur Dorros' *Ant Cities*, and *Beastly Neighbors* by Mollie Rights.

2. Walk around outside to find ant colonies.

3. Observe the insects and their mounds with magnifying glass.

4. Make sure no one harms ants or their habitat.

5. Carefully spoon a single ant into a sealable bag and examine it with a magnifying glass.

6. Discuss the parts of an ant such as the head, thorax, abdomen, jointed legs, compound eyes, and antennae.

7. Draw a picture of the ant with the details seen under the magnifying glass.

8. When the observations are complete, return all ants to their natural habitat.

9. As a follow-up activity, you might consider purchasing an ant farm (or see activity H7).

ANIMALS:
Ants' Favorite Foods (I5)

Materials:

- ❑ paper plate
- ❑ marker

- ❑ variety of food (honey, meat, peanut butter, grass, moldy leaves, etc.)

Directions:

1. Mark off a paper plate into 6 or 8 parts using a marker.

2. Place small portions of food into each section.

3. Record kids' predictions of which foods will attract the most ants.

4. Place the plate near an ant colony.

5. Observe the plate throughout the day to see which foods are eaten and how much.

6. Watch the path the ants travel.

7. Also observe how the size of the food portion affects what the ant will take.

ANIMALS:
Animal Scavenger Hunt (16)

Materials:

❑ paper   ❑ pencil

Directions:

1.   If possible, have books on animals and the regions of the world they live in.

2.   Have kids brainstorm a list of different animals.

3.   Make predictions of which animals they could find outside.

4.   Go on a nature hike and see how many you can find.

5.   What animals did you find that were not on your list?

6.   What animals did you see the most? Why do you think that animal was so common?

7.   Would it be different at night?

8.   Discuss which animals on your list you didn't find. Why?

ANIMALS:
In Disguise (17)

Materials:

- ❏ green construction paper
- ❏ brown construction paper
- ❏ yellow construction paper
- ❏ red construction paper

Directions:

1. This activity will be done outside.

2. Have children cut out or tear 100 pieces of each color paper.

3. Paper pieces should then be scattered outside in a grassy, preferably wooded, area.

4. Children will then pretend they are birds and the paper pieces are insects.

5. Kids try to find as many pieces of paper as possible in one minute.

6. Afterward, discuss which color kids would prefer to be if they were an insect. Why?

7. How would this change in other environments (the dessert, the beach, etc.)?

ANIMALS:
Casting Animal Tracks (I8)

Materials:

- Brush
- Eye dropper
- Cardboard, plastic, or wood

strips (plastic is best)
- Paper clip
- Plaster of Paris

Directions:

1. Find animal tracks. The easiest to preserve are those in mud, wet ground, or snow.

2. Brush away debris from area using a brush or stiff piece of grass. Use an eye dropper to remove any water in the track.

3. Make a frame around track with the strips. Plastic works best because you can easily shape it in a circle around the track.

4. Clip the ends of the strips together with a paper clip.

5. Add 2 parts plaster to 5 parts water. The plaster should be the consistency of thick cream.

6. Pour plaster gently into frame. The cast will need to be at least ¾ of an inch thick.

7. It will take roughly 30 minutes for the cast to dry.

8. Once cast is dry, carefully remove the cast. It may still take a few days for cast to completely harden.

Source: http://bizarrelabs.com/track.htm

ANIMALS:
Adopt an Animal (I9)

Materials:

- ❑ resource books about animals
- ❑ paper
- ❑ pencil
- ❑ markers
- ❑ folder

Directions:

1. First, contact your local zoo and see if they have an "Adopt-an-Animal" program. If there is a cost that is too much for you to handle, see if they can at least provide written materials about animals.

2. Let the kids pick an animal to adopt.

3. Use the resource books to learn as much as you can about that animal.

4. You can encourage the kids to write about the animals or draw pictures of the animal and its habitat and store everything in a folder.

CAMPING

CAMPING:
Pitch a Tent (J1)

Materials:

- ❏ Tents
- ❏ Blankets
- ❏ Pillows
- ❏ Sleeping bags

Directions:

1. Pitching a tent on your program grounds can make for hours of entertainment. Put the word out to families that you would like to borrow some tents and let the families know how long you will need the tents.

2. Tents come in a wide variety of style and complexity. Make sure you understand what kind of tent you've got and how difficult it will be to set up. You might even enlist parents' help in setting up tents.

3. Depending on the difficulty in setting up tents, engage the kids in the process as much as possible. Some tents can be pitched without stakes. These are great for indoor or outdoor play.

4. Once tents are set up, you can line the floor of the tent with blankets, pillows, and sleeping bags.

CAMPING:
Build a Campfire (J2)

Materials:

- ❑ Paper towel tubes
- ❑ Tissue paper - red, orange, and yellow
- ❑ Rocks
- ❑ Carpet squares

Directions:

1. Create a campfire for dramatic play indoors or outdoors by using paper towel tubes for logs.

2. Use crumbled up yellow, red, and orange tissue paper to simulate the fire.

3. Use real rocks to make a circle around the fire.

4. You can then also put carpet squares around the fire for a story time.

Source:
http://www.childfun.com/modules.php?name=News&file=article&sid=161

CAMPING:
Pack a Backpack (J3)

Materials:

❑ Backpacks ❑ Materials for packing

Directions:

1. Talk to kids about what you would need if you went camping and had to carry everything on your back.

2. When doing so, ask kids what they need for:
   - sleeping (sleeping bag, blankets, pillows)
   - clothing (consider weather changes when it is nighttime or it rains or snows)
   - food (what foods can be carried easily and prepared easily?)
   - cooking (what kinds of pots and pans and utensils do you need?)
   - protection from nature (bug spray, sun screen, etc.)
   - playing and fun (remember - no electricity!)

3. Talk to kids about how important it is to pack lightly if you have to carry everything on your back.

4. Also, talk about how long this hike would be. Where would it be?

5. Finally, have plenty of materials on hand for kids to pack the backpack and try walking with it to see how heavy it would be.

6. The backpack and its contents can also make for a great prop to go with a tent (see activity I1).

CAMPING:
Nature Tapes (J4)

Materials:

❑ Tape recorder (with recording capabilities)

❑ Blank cassettes

Directions:

1. There are plenty of CDs available of pre-recorded nature sounds, such as rain forests, babbling brooks, etc. However, what kinds of nature sounds can the kids find?

2. Let kids have access to a tape recorder and tapes.

3. Go on a hike outdoors and tape the sounds that you hear.

4. Remind kids that to truly capture the sounds of nature, they will have to be quiet. Consequently, this is best as a small group activity.

5. After kids make the tapes, they can listen to them and see if they can identify the different nature sounds that they hear. In addition, what sounds do they hear that are not from nature?

6. Finally, the nature tapes can also be used in a camping area set up indoors or outdoors.

CAMPING:
Mapping and Orienteering (J5)

Materials:

- ❑ Plain paper
- ❑ Graph paper
- ❑ Writing instruments
- ❑ Tape measures
- ❑ String
- ❑ Compass

Directions:

1. Kids can make maps outdoors with just paper and pencil. For younger kids, it may just be fun to draw objects that they see outdoors.

2. However, older kids can try to make their maps to scale. Kids can use several methods for finding how far apart objects are, including tape measures, string, and pacing off steps.

3. If kids want to make something more on the order of a treasure map for other kids to follow, they can use a compass as well. Encourage kids to write directions like "Start at the large oak tree by the swings. Take 5 paces Northwest."

CAMPING:
Fishing (J6)

Materials:

- Egg carton
- String
- Paper clips
- S-shaped styrofoam pieces
- Paper

- Paint
- Other decorative materials
- Magnets
- Sticks
- String

Directions:

1. Make a tackle box with an egg carton. Poke holes on either end and tie string to make a handle. Kids can then decorate as they wish.

2. Use paper clips for hooks and S-shaped styrofoam pieces as the worms.

3. You can also glue magnets to fish that kids cut out. Then tie string to the sticks and attach the paper clip hooks and see if you can attach them to the magnet fish. You may have to experiment with different kinds of "hooks" and magnets to make sure it works.

Source: Adapted from
http://www.childfun.com/modules.php?name=News&file=article&sid=161

CAMPING:
First Aid Kit Necklace (J7)

Materials:

- ❑ Film canister
- ❑ Yarn
- ❑ small packet of antiseptic wipe or alcohol
- ❑ Bandaids
- ❑ Safety pin

- ❑ Small wrapped hard candy
- ❑ Money for a phone call
- ❑ Piece of paper with important phone numbers
- ❑ Red nail polish

Directions:

1. Put holes in the sides of the film container, and attach a long piece of yarn to go around the neck.

2. You can also poke a hole in lid; feed one end of the yarn through the hole; thread that end through a pony bead; and then push the end of the yarn back through the hole.

3. Tie yarn into a knot so it is snug against the film container lid. Tie another knot in yarn to around your neck.

4. Fill film canister with first aid supplies.

5. Paint a red cross on the outside with nail polish.

Source: http://familycrafts.about.com/cs/miscjewelry/a/blfcfirstaidn.htm

CAMPING:
Homemade Mosquito Repellant
(J8)

- ❑ 1/3 cup apple-cider vinegar
- ❑ 1/3 cup witch hazel
- ❑ 5 drops citronella oil (can be found at health food stores)
- ❑ Spoon
- ❑ Paint pens
- ❑ Small spray bottle

Directions:

1. Pour all ingredients in a spray bottle.

2. Shake well each time before you spray. The vinegar smell will go away quickly.

3. Decorate bottle as desired.

Source: http://clk.about.com

TAKING CARE OF OUR WORLD

TAKING CARE OF OUR WORLD:
Clean Up Time (K1)

Materials:

❑ trash bags

Directions:

1. Children should work in small groups or pairs, each group with a trash bag.

2. Warn children not to pick up broken glass.

3. Have kids collect trash outdoors.

4. Have children divide trash into categories (paper, aluminum, plastic, etc.).

5. Which category has the most trash? Why?

6. What could be done to cut down on trash?

7. What can be done to keep the environment clean?

TAKING CARE OF OUR WORLD:
Invention Convention (K2)

Materials:

- unlimited supply of recycled items
- Paper
- pencil
- variety of materials for attaching items (string, staples, glue, tape, etc.)

Directions:

1. Kids can work alone or in groups.

2. With the materials available, they should develop an idea of a product to make.

3. Design the product first on paper, detailing what it does and what is needed to make it.

4. Once designed, they may make the product.

5. When products are complete, kids can create displays and put on an "Invention Convention" where they show off their products to each other and share how they work.

TAKING CARE OF OUR WORLD:
Recycle Drive (K3)

Materials:

- ❑ large boxes or containers
- ❑ markers
- ❑ paper
- ❑ tape

Directions:

1. Kids can run their own recycle drive by putting out various containers and boxes and labeling them with categories such as glass, plastic, newspaper, etc.

2. They can also make posters to advertise their recycle drive. The posters should indicate where to bring supplies, what to bring, and when materials can be collected.

3. Make sure to check first where recyclables can be taken once they are collected (and what exactly can be taken).

TAKING CARE OF OUR WORLD:
Toy Drive (K4)

Materials:

- ❑ large boxes
- ❑ poster board
- ❑ markers

Directions:

1. Find a local charity which accepts toy donations. Make sure you know what their guidelines are (for example, they may not take toys with broken parts, missing pieces, or multiple pieces).

2. Make signs explaining when the toy drive is and where people can drop off toys.

3. Decorate the large boxes and post any necessary directions on them regarding what kinds of toys can be collected.

4. Once toys have been collected, kids can help "test" them to make sure they meet the guidelines for the charity for which you are collecting the toys.

5. Finally, the toys can be delivered to the charity.

TAKING CARE OF OUR WORLD:
Recycled Needs Chart (K5)

Materials:

- ❑ large piece of poster board
- ❑ matte knife
- ❑ markers
- ❑ ruler
- ❑ large box

Directions:

1. Cut small slits on poster board into which smaller strips of paper can be inserted.

2. On the strips of paper, children write various recyclables needed for upcoming projects.

3. Decorate a box for donations to go in.

4. The poster should be posted at the parent sign-in/out area along with the box.

TAKING CARE OF OUR WORLD:
Recycled Paper (K6)

Materials:

- ❑ 2 1/2 single pages of newspaper
- ❑ whole section of a newspaper
- ❑ big square pan at least 3 inches deep
- ❑ blender
- ❑ window screen fit to pan
- ❑ measuring cup
- ❑ flat piece of wood the size of a newspaper

Directions:

1. Tear 2 ½ pages into tiny pieces. Mix into a blender with 5 cups water.

2. Cover blender and turn on a few seconds until paper turns to pulp.

3. Pour about 1 inch of water into pan.

4. Put screen in pan and pour 1 cup paper pulp on the screen. Spread evenly. Lift screen and let water drain.

5. Place screen with pulp in the middle of the newspaper section and close it back.

6. Flip the newspaper over so that the screen will be on top of the pulp.

7. Place board on top and press to get rid of excess water.

8. Take out screen and leave newspaper open for 24 hours to let pulp dry.

9. The next day you should be able to write on your newspaper.

TAKING CARE OF OUR WORLD:
Facility Checklist (K7)

Materials:

❑ Computer with internet access

Directions:

1. Kids can create a checklist for your facility to determine where waste can be cut and resources can be used more efficiently.

2. Get kids to brainstorm ways where these things can be done. Consider:
   - Does your facility recycle?
   - Does it have a compost heap?
   - Are its lightbulbs energy efficient?
   - Are lights turned off when not in use?
   - Are there any leaky faucets?
   - How much paper is generated in office areas? Is paper reused when possible?

3. The source link below offers several links to school-based projects which will offer ideas for what kinds of things can be inspected at the school.

4. Let kids report findings to whoever is in charge of your facility. You should discuss the project with this person beforehand to make sure he/she will be receptive.

Source: http://www.kidsrecycle.org/kids_links.php

INDEX

131

RESOURCES

Throughout these cards, resources are cited when known. Some projects in this set have probably been passed around, but owe their origin to a specific unknown source. If you are aware of a source that isn't cited, please let Toolbox Training know! Meanwhile, here are other resources to check out:

❑ Allcrafts.net/nature.htm

❑ http://bizarrelabs.com. (2007). Compiled by Brian Carusella.

❑ Carlson, Laurie. (1995). *Kids Camp!: Activities for the Backyard or Wilderness.* Chicago Review Press.

❑ The Earth Works Group. (1990). *50 Simple Things Kids Can Do to Save the Earth.* Andrews and McMeel: Kansas City, MO.

❑ http://fun.familyeducation.com

❑ Koonz, Robin Michal. (1998). *The Complete Backyard Nature Activity Book: Fun Projects for Kids to Learn About the Wonders of Wildlife and Nature.* McGraw-Hill.

❑ Milord, Susan. (1996). *The Kids' Nature Book: 365 Indoor/Outdoor Activities and Experiences.* Williamson Publishing Company.

❑ Petrash, Carol. (1992). *Earthways: Simple Environmental Activities for Young Children.* Gryphon House.

❑ VanCleave, Janice. (1991). *Earth Science for Every Kid.* John Wiley & Sons: New York, NY.

❑ Williams, Joy. (2002). *Nature Crafts.* North Light Books.

About the Author and TOOLBOX TRAINING

David Whitaker entered the child care field in 1987. He has worked as a trainer, consultant, author, program coordinator, and lead teacher in various facilities (school, church, center, recreation) with preschoolers, kindergartners, school-agers, and middle school-age kids in half-day, full-day, before-and-after, and summer

programs. He served on the MOSAC2 (Missouri School-Age Care Coalition) and Missouri Accreditation (MoA) state boards as well as the Parents As Teachers Family Network board. He has a Masters in Education and taught for the School-Age Care degree program at Concordia University in St. Paul, MN. He formed TOOLBOX TRAINING in January 1998 to create tools to improve the quality of child care. Check out www.toolboxtrainingonline.com for more details on any of the below.

Workshops and Training Packages: A wide variety of TOOLBOX TRAINING workshops are available for delivery right at your program. Topics include discipline, parent communication, lesson planning, games, multiple intelligences, and transition activities. All workshops are also available as ready-to-use training packages that let you conduct a workshop yourself.

Books and Activity Cards: In addition to training packages, TOOLBOX TRAINING offers books on topics such as multiple intelligences, transition activities, and games. In addition, there are various sets of activity cards, each offering 100 simple-to-do activities in categories such as art, games, science, nature, drama, and music.

Connecting with Others in the Field: Check out TOOLBOX TRAINING on Facebook (www.facebook.com/toolboxtraining) to join discussions with others in the profession. Also, if you have comments on any activities in this book or ideas have been sparked that you'd like to share, go to "Discussions" on the Facebook page and click on the appropriate topic heading. See you there!